Rejoice and Be Glad

Daily Reflections for Easter to Pentecost 2020

Mary DeTurris Poust

LITURGICAL PRESS

Collegeville, Minnesota

www.litpress.org

Nihil Obstat: Reverend Robert Harren, J.C.L., *Censor deputatus.*
Imprimatur: ✠ Most Reverend Donald J. Kettler, J.C.L., Bishop of Saint Cloud, May 31, 2019.

Cover design by Monica Bokinskie. Cover art courtesy of Getty Images.

ISSN: 2578-7004 (Print)
ISSN: 2578-7012 (Online)

ISBN: 978-0-8146-6367-7   978-0-8146-6392-9 (e-book)

Introduction

On the weekend I had planned to write the introduction to this book of reflections, I sat down with my laptop and nothing came out. I rarely find myself in the position of having nothing to say (just ask my family and friends). But on this day, it felt like a message. I wasn't ready. I needed more time to think, to pray, to reflect, and so I put the computer away.

That evening, Chiara, the youngest of my three children, returned home from an overnight at the New York State varsity gymnastics meet. When she set down her bag, I could see wilted branches wrapped in cellophane. I asked her what it was. She pulled out the sad bouquet and handed it to me, saying how they were pretty at the start of the day. Undeterred by their more-dead-than-alive appearance, I dug out a small vase, filled it with fresh water, trimmed off the bottoms of the stems, and set the maroon and white flowers on the counter. Both Chiara and my husband, Dennis, looked at me like I was a little crazy. The flowers were so completely drooped over it was the most pathetic flower arrangement I'd ever seen. And still, I insisted that a little water would revive them.

When I came downstairs the next morning, the flowers greeted me, looking as beautiful and alive as they must have when they were freshly cut. I smiled and turned to the review copy of a book I'd been asked to "blurb," not thinking much more about the flowers. As I read the very first meditation in this yet-to-be-published manuscript about finding our spiritual teachers all around us, I read these words: "Ask the plants of the earth, and they will teach you . . ." And I stopped short as if someone had just hit me in the head with a brick and turned around to look at the flowers again as if they might actually speak to me. That's when I knew I'd been waiting for this moment to write this introduction.

Those flowers on my counter—and probably countless things dotting the counters and corners of your own life right now—are reminders that Easter is always all around us, even when we think there is no hope, even when we think all is lost. Jesus tells us today, this season, there is always reason to look forward in faith because he has defeated death for our sake and nothing can steal our salvation if we turn to God in trust and put one foot in front of the other on the journey of The Way day after day.

Jesus is the spiritual water that refreshes us, that takes our drooping spirits and revives us, that gives us new life when we think we can't go on. Today is the first day of our Easter season, of the rest of our lives. Writing these reflections was truly a gift. Year after year, I focus on the readings of Lent (or Advent), but this journey allowed me to spend time on less-traveled paths through the daily details of the Acts of the Apostles and other Easter-season readings. I hope you, too, will find something new in these familiar stories, something that will pour fresh water on your soul and bring you back to life.

Reflections

April 12: Easter Sunday of the Resurrection of the Lord

Rain or Shine

Readings: Acts 10:34a, 37-43; Col 3:1-4 or 1 Cor 5:6b-8; John 20:1-9 or Matt 28:1-10

Scripture:
"He is not here, for he has been raised just as he said." (Matt 28:6)

Reflection: Easter brings back powerful memories of my teen years, when I was a leader in our parish Catholic Youth Organization. Several years running, we planned a sunrise Easter Mass. We baked our own Communion bread (according to an official recipe, of course). We made felt banners (it was the late 70s, after all) and we planned and practiced music. And, inevitably, it would rain and Mass would end up in the small cinderblock chapel at our parish, which had no church building at the time. But that did nothing to dampen our Easter joy. We were so filled with the Spirit and so ready to sing "Alleluia" that rain and cold and concrete had no effect. Jesus had risen from the dead. How could we possibly be disappointed?

No matter where you find yourself today, whatever your problems and struggles, whatever your plans and responsibilities, there is reason to rejoice. Jesus is not dead; he is alive. The cross was not defeat for him, and it will not be defeat for us if we put our trust in him. We do not always understand Jesus' ways. Like those early disciples, we may stare at the empty tomb—or at some other challenge in our own life—and wonder, "How can this be?" Jesus doesn't ask us to understand; he asks us to trust that things are unfolding just as he said.

Meditation: When you go to Mass today, pay attention to your physical surroundings—the Paschal candle flickering, the lilies with their powerful fragrance, the music bursting with Alleluias, the children in patent-leather shoes, the incense rising toward heaven, the holy water cold against your skin, a shower of blessings in the most literal sense. It's beautiful the way we use physical things to help us bridge the distance to God, as though we are so hungry to get closer, we pull out all the stops. If only we could keep that fire of love going year-round. The Church gives us a running start by offering us this beautiful fifty-day season of Easter. We might not wear Easter bonnets every week, but the water and candles, music and joy will be present in the liturgy. Soak it up. Let it feed your soul.

Prayer: Alleluia, Alleluia! He is risen! We sing out with joy, we bow down in gratitude, we rejoice in the resurrection.

Facing Fear

Readings: Acts 2:14, 22-33; Matt 28:8-15

Scripture:
Mary Magdalene and the other Mary went away quickly from the tomb, fearful yet overjoyed. (Matt 28:8)

Reflection: Fearful yet overjoyed. That could probably describe a lot of moments in our lives. For me, it conjures up powerful and precious memories of childbirth—the anticipation of wanting to meet my baby, coupled with the fear of labor. Still, after each of my three children were born, how quickly the fear faded from memory leaving only softness in its place. I imagine for the women at the tomb, the experience in today's Gospel was much the same, as the fear of Good Friday, still so fresh in their minds, is replaced with the realization that He is risen. They did not know what to make of it, and yet they knew enough to run and spread the news.

Maybe that's why Jesus appeared first to the women. Because he knew that those fearless enough to sacrifice everything to bring new life into the world were sure to be fearless in the face of the impossible. Rather than hide, the women rejoiced; rather than question, the women believed. How easy it would have been to brush aside their encounter as a figment of the imagination, grief pangs taken to the extreme.

But they chose the more difficult path: the path of truth, the Way of Jesus. And they were not content to keep it to themselves. They knew they had to share the Good News of Jesus Christ with all who would listen. Will we choose the same?

Meditation: Think of a time in your life when you felt both fear and joy. Was it a new job, a new child, a move to another city, a relationship that required risk? What made joy win out over fear? Now think of a time in your life when fear made you shrink back, left you paralyzed. What did you do to shake out of it? Where was God in the midst of it? Was God obviously present, or perhaps only visible in hindsight? Today, let go of any fear that is holding you back, and, like the women at the tomb, let the joy of Easter flood your heart and shake you out of your spiritual slumber.

Prayer: Risen Jesus, give us the courage to live with joy even when we are afraid, to know you are with us even when we feel alone, to take your message out into the world where it can heal, comfort, strengthen, save.

The Garden of Our Lives

Readings: Acts 2:36-41; John 20:11-18

Scripture:
"Woman, why are you weeping? Whom are you looking for?" (John 20:15)

Reflection: I love the image of Jesus as gardener in today's Gospel. Mary Magdalene, finding the tomb empty, is looking for her Master, unaware that he is right there in front of her, hidden in plain sight, until he speaks her name and her eyes are opened, there in a garden. What she thought was lost was there all the time. What she thought had been taken from her is suddenly so real that Jesus must tell her not to hold onto him. I have to admit that this is one of my favorite scenes in the Bible, maybe my most favorite. It's the reading I really want to hear on Easter morning because to me it is the essence of the resurrection realization moment and a reminder that the first witness to Jesus' glorified body was not one of the twelve but Mary of Magdala, the woman who would come to be known as the Apostle to the Apostles. The one who is the first to announce: "I have seen the Lord."

What if Mary hadn't happened down that path that day? What if, out of fear, she opted not to follow through with the burial rituals and responsibilities left to the women to handle? The apostles were hiding, afraid their faith might mark them for the same violent end as their teacher. What if Mary had not been able to recognize her name when it was spoken by the Lord because she was distracted by fear or too timid to confront the gardener with her questions?

Meditation: Where are the gardens in your life, the places you've wandered in search of something important—purpose, love, faith, courage—and found only emptiness or what you thought was a void? You might connect that search with an actual physical location: the beach, a mountain, a chapel. Maybe it's an internal landscape where you seek meaning amid the chatter of your worried mind. Just be still for a moment. Enter into silence and listen. Where is the Lord calling you? Maybe he was right there all the time. Turn toward him, as Mary did, and face this beautiful truth.

Prayer: We are searching for you, Lord, in the busyness of our lives, the solitude of our struggles, the chaos of our world. Help us to hear your voice, to see your face there in the garden of our lives.

Sensing Something Special

Readings: Acts 3:1-10; Luke 24:13-35

Scripture:
"Oh, how foolish you are! How slow of heart to believe all that the prophets spoke!" (Luke 24:25)

Reflection: For the third day in a row, our readings take us inside the fear and confusion that existed in the days immediately following Jesus' death on the cross. Today, as the two men walk on the road to Emmaus talking to the stranger, we can feel their frustration, desperation, and disappointment. Jesus, who was supposed to save them, save all of Israel, was crucified! You can imagine them talking animatedly, arms waving, as they tried to make the stranger understand the enormity of their grief.

Even as Jesus scolds them for their foolishness and interprets the words of the prophets, they cannot see past his appearance to the reality of the Messiah walking alongside them. But they do sense something. What is it? What about this man makes them say, "Stay with us"? While they may not recognize him, it's clear that they recognize something in his words. He gives them comfort and stability at a time when they are reeling. And Jesus is ever patient with them, waiting for them to come to their senses and see his promise made manifest. It takes the breaking of the bread to do that.

The meal that has become the heart of the message opens their eyes, and all the fear and confusion drops away. Like the women before them, they come to understand, finally, that Jesus has defeated death, defeated the cross, and won for all of them, all of us, salvation.

Meditation: We hear the stories of Scripture so often over the course of our lives that we can become numb to the meaning. Like the disciples walking along the road to Emmaus, we can hear the Word and still miss God present in the midst of it. What would it take to make the message stick, to open our eyes to the ways we've been living outside the bounds of the Gospel, choosing comfort over compassion, ease over truth? Throughout this season, as the familiar Scriptures repeat, try to see them in a new light. Find a phrase, a scene, a word, and stay there for a while. Let it work its way into a tiny crack in your armor.

Prayer: Word of God, we look to you today and every day for guidance and growth. We know you have the words of everlasting life. Help us to hear them with our hearts and live them through our actions.

Open Minds, Open Hearts

Readings: Acts 3:11-26; Luke 24:35-48

Scripture:
"Why are you troubled? And why do questions arise in your hearts?" (Luke 24:38)

Reflection: Believing in something we can't see isn't always easy. As it turns out, even seeing isn't always enough for believing, at least not at first. With Jesus standing in their midst, the apostles struggled to wrap their minds around the resurrection. They were troubled, and who can blame them? Jesus can see the questions on their faces; he knows he is asking them to accept the impossible, or what had been impossible up until that day. Jesus has to "open their minds" to the Scripture. Only then can they accept his dying and rising and believe so fervently that they then go out and preach it, even at the risk of their own safety.

Sometimes I wish I could have a moment like that, where Jesus opens my mind and everything makes sense. The questions that rise in my heart day after day would vanish and suddenly there would be a great *aha!* I don't see that happening any time soon, and so I am often troubled—troubled by what I can't understand, troubled that my belief is not strong enough, troubled that I'll never get it right before I leave this world for the next. And through it all, if I stop my swirling and stressing, Jesus asks, "Why?"

Why are you troubled? Jesus is here. Right now. Look at his wounds and see your salvation.

Meditation: My grandmother used to love to do the old "Jumble" puzzles that ran in the newspaper. She enjoyed the challenge of trying to make sense out of something nonsensical. Have you ever been stumped by a puzzle? For me it's always been Rubik's cube, and yet I have a cousin who can solve that puzzle in under a minute. I think our spiritual lives can fall into similar patterns. We often struggle to put everything in its place and make order out of chaos. Some of us can cut right through the madness and get to the heart of the matter; others of us make false starts, backtrack, get lost, but always with our eyes on heaven. There is no need to be troubled. The puzzle will solve itself when we trust God completely and the scales fall from our eyes.

Prayer: God of miracles and wonders, open our minds to your word, to your presence, to your truth. Clear away the clouds of confusion so that we may focus fully on you.

Standing Strong

Readings: Acts 4:1-12; John 21:1-14

Scripture:
But many of those who heard the word came to believe and the number of men grew to about five thousand. (Acts 4:4)

Reflection: Whenever I feel doubt creeping into my faith life, I come back to the one thing that tends to drive the doubt away: people throughout history, from the scene in today's Gospel right up until today, have been willing to suffer rather than lose their faith. Those who knew Jesus firsthand were willing to risk abuse, imprisonment, even death in order to spread the Gospel. Peter, who once denied even knowing Jesus and who later dies a martyr's death on a cross, in today's reading defiantly says that it is in Jesus' name that he has cured a crippled man. But even beyond that already remarkable fact, he tells them that there is no salvation except through Jesus. That must have been both frightening and infuriating to the Jewish leaders at the time. This Jesus whom they tried to destroy had not gone away after all; his strength and reach was growing exponentially day by day, all fueled by one key ingredient: love, for God and for neighbor.

What would we be willing to do in Jesus' name? Chances are we'd probably like the idea of curing someone who is ill through faith, but that kind of discipleship comes at a price.

Whether it's the ultimate sacrifice of outright persecution or the sacrifice of leaving home to serve the poor or simply the sacrifice of trying to live the Gospel as we raise a family, faith in Jesus costs something, and it should. Are we willing to accept what faith requires, even when that means discomfort, challenge, humiliation, and maybe, in the most extreme cases, physical suffering? Would we be as confidant and defiant as Peter if someone were to confront us and ask us in whose name we do our work and have our being?

Meditation: Does your faith ever cause you discomfort? At work or in social circles? Among friends or relatives? Have you ever felt afraid to speak the truth of the Gospel due to fear of humiliation or a verbal challenge? The next time that happens, rather than focus on the thing that makes you afraid, focus on the thing that brings you joy. When you share the joy of your faith, there is nothing to fear.

Prayer: Spirit of God, give us the courage to speak the truth not only through our words but through our actions. Let our faith draw others to you.

Seeing Isn't Always Believing

Readings: Acts 4:13-21; Mark 16:9-15

Scripture:
[Later on,] he appeared in another form to two of them walking along on their way to the country. (Mark 16:12)

Reflection: Isn't it interesting that every time Jesus appears to his disciples in the days following the resurrection, his identity is hidden at first? In the garden, on the road to Emmaus, in the locked upper room. The disciples don't immediately recognize Jesus, and those who haven't seen for themselves refuse to believe the reports. Only after something remarkable happens, do they realize it is Jesus. That gives me some comfort. Even Jesus' closest followers had a hard time seeing and believing. They needed a nudge, a miracle, a sign. Or, in today's case, being "taken to task" by the Master himself.

How often do we go about our days missing God's presence in our lives? We pray for a sign, we ask God to speak to us, we wander through our days in a spiritual haze, not noticing or recognizing the miraculous among the mundane moments of our lives. All the while Jesus is there, hoping that at some point we will recognize him, hoping we will want to stay near him always, hoping our belief will compel us to want to share that same peace and joy with others. But we are not so easily transformed, are we? We are a fickle lot, but Jesus is patient, persistent, present.

Meditation: Has there ever been a time in your life when, after something amazing happened, you thought back and only then recognized God's hand in it? I remember a time years ago, when I had told someone in passing that I wished God would write me a letter and tell me what I needed to do. In the week that followed, I received a bunch of unexpected handwritten letters from friends (all of them strangers to each other) who decided to write me encouraging words out of the blue. I didn't see the connection until the fourth day when two letters showed up at once. And at that moment, it was as though my eyes had been opened for the first time, as though the colors around me were suddenly brighter, deeper. I was transformed, or so I thought. But a few weeks later, I was back to the usual whining, waiting for another sign. The brilliant colors hadn't faded; only my faith had.

Prayer: God of mystery, help us to recognize you in the details of our daily lives, to see your face in those walking this journey around us, and to react with joy and with love.

April 19: Second Sunday of Easter
(Sunday of Divine Mercy)

Tested by Fire

Readings: Acts 2:42-47; 1 Pet 1:3-9; John 20:19-31

Scripture:
Blessed be the God and Father of our Lord Jesus Christ, who in his great mercy gave us a new birth to a living hope through the resurrection of Jesus Christ from the dead. (1 Pet 1:3)

Reflection: Suffering and mercy, doubt and faith are front and center in today's readings, from Thomas' infamous moment in the upper room, to Peter's warning of the trials that will come to test the faith of Jesus' followers, to the Gospel that offers us a glimpse of the forgiveness that is ours through the sacrament of reconciliation. One week after Easter, the lilies still vibrant, the joy still sweet, and already we have returned to themes that make us a little uncomfortable. Can't we revel in this resurrection celebration a little while longer before talking about suffering and trials?

That's seeing the Easter news with worldly eyes, eyes that look away at the first hint of difficulty and discomfort, strain and struggle. We want faith to bring us a peace that promises ease and calm, but if the cross teaches us anything it's that ease is not the way of a disciple. And, really, when you think about it, how many truly worthwhile things in your life were easy to attain? None, I'm guessing. This journey through life will take us high and low, through fields of flowers and deserts of scorched earth. But always Jesus is with us, offering the cooling waters of forgiveness, renewal, mercy, and hope. On this Divine Mercy Sunday, let us ponder the image of Jesus with water and blood pouring from his wounded side and know in our souls that his suffering washes us clean and offers salvation, and say with confidence, "Jesus, I trust in you."

Meditation: We all have a little Thomas in us. No matter how strong our faith, there's a piece of us that harbors a sliver of doubt, especially when things take a turn for the worse or some trial makes us wonder. Poor Thomas gets a bad rap for his doubt, but can you blame him? Believing that Jesus was back from the dead was too good to be true. We've probably known that feeling, hearing something through the grapevine and thinking, "I'll believe it when I see it." Jesus reminds us today that being able to believe without seeing is a gift. Today, renew your trust in Jesus' promise.

Prayer: God of mercy, we trust in your goodness, even when our human hearts are overcome by the shadow of doubt. Give us faith that requires no proof, that withstands any test.

Earth, Wind and Fire

Readings: Acts 4:23-31; John 3:1-8

Scripture:
"The wind blows where it wills, and you can hear the sound it makes, but you do not know where it comes from or where it goes; so it is with everyone who is born of the Spirit." (John 3:8)

Reflection: When someone says he is "born again," it has certain connotations in our society, and for those of us who are Catholic, it can seem somewhat mysterious or strange. But Jesus tells us quite plainly in today's Gospel that none of us are getting to heaven unless we are born again, or, more accurately, "born from above." (John 3:3) We don't have to speak in tongues or walk on nails or stand on street corners quoting Scripture. What Jesus is describing is at once powerful and invisible, earth-shattering and quiet as a whisper. Imagine a breeze barely moving a curtain hanging in an open window. You might catch it out of the corner of your eye, but, more likely, you'd miss it. That doesn't mean the breeze isn't there. Would we notice the Spirit if we were moved in such a way, or would we be so distracted, so busy that we'd miss the nudge and with it the chance to be reborn?

Sometimes I think we close the window on the Spirit because we're afraid of what being born from above might mean, afraid to get too close to that kind of transforming power. We might not even realize we're doing it. It's instinctual. We want to protect our comfortable routine, and Spirit is anything but comfortable or routine. Being born again requires boldness, as we see in the first reading when the Spirit's presence is so powerful the earth shakes. Are you willing to let yourself be shaken up by the Spirit in order to be saved?

Meditation: Being born again sounds like quite a task. Where do we begin? In prayer. Always in prayer. And in silence. Keep bringing yourself back to stillness today. When you feel yourself starting to spin your wheels, come back to your center. If you have a short prayer that can help you do that, use that method. Say the one-line Jesus prayer: "Lord, Jesus Christ, Son of God, have mercy on me a sinner." Or pare it down even more and just say simply, "Mercy." Maybe there's another phrase or word that helps quiet your soul. Use it daily until it helps open up a space in you where the Spirit can enter.

Prayer: Breath of God, carry me along on the current of your love until my heart is blazing with the spiritual fire that comes from trusting you completely.

Imperfect Harmony

Readings: Acts 4:32-37; John 3:7b-15

Scripture:
The community of believers was of one heart and mind, and no one claimed that any of his possessions was his own, but they had everything in common. (Acts 4:32)

Reflection: I don't know about you, but I can't even get the community of believers around my own kitchen table to be of one heart and mind on most days. So I'm in awe of the way the community in today's first reading managed to create harmony in a world that was anything but harmonious. Persecution and peril were around every corner, but these earliest Christians were so committed to the teachings of Jesus that their differences faded away or were at least kept under control. That's a far cry from the world we live in, where nothing seems to be under control and everything is a reason to take sides and join in the shouting match, whether virtual or literal.

While we are often willing to donate money to those in need, to volunteer our time for a good cause, and to come together at least once a week to worship, that kind of compartmentalized Gospel living allows us to be our brother's keeper without being our brother's brother (or sister). Obviously, not all of us are going to sell our homes and throw the funds into a mutual pot and live as one big happy family, but what if we start building harmonious Christian community right where we are?

Meditation: Spiritual writer and theologian Henri Nouwen often wrote about the importance of community in the spiritual life, saying, "We witness to God's compassionate presence in the world by the way we live and work together." But for many of us, living and working with others is precisely where we find stress and tension. How can we begin to live and work with others in a way that fosters compassion and harmony over discord and disappointment? Even if we don't share everything in common like our earliest spiritual forbears, can we take a cue from them and find ways to pray together in common at home, to instill, if not overtly spiritual, at least emotionally supportive actions in our workplaces, to help build up the communal prayer life of our parishes not just on Sunday but throughout the week and year? What's one thing you can do today to take the first step toward building Christian community?

Prayer: God of compassion, teach us to bear our differences in patience and love, to let petty slights go, and to focus instead on the deeper things that bind us together as a human family.

Cover of Darkness

Readings: Acts 5:17-26; John 3:16-21

Scripture:
And this is the verdict, that the light came into the world, but people preferred darkness to light, because their works were evil. (John 3:19)

Reflection: We have seen all too well in our Church what happens when people prefer darkness to light. The scandal that continues, like a millstone around the neck of our universal Church, happened because people feared the light and what the light might reveal and how that might reflect on them, even if they weren't the ones doing the evil deeds, abusing the children. And so, all these years later, the faithful have had to grapple again and again with the failed humanity that is our Church, with the darkness that continues to exert its power even among those who have been entrusted with passing on the faith, with forgiving sins, with celebrating Mass and giving us Eucharist. It can be hard for the people in the pews to take, this repeating, enveloping darkness that robs them of the trust they once had.

Darkness is seductive, and not in a sensual way. It feels safe and comfortable, like a blanket protecting us against a chill. But in actuality, it is dangerous, devilish because it lets us forget about the things we don't want to admit or don't like to look at. If we avoid the light of truth, the light of Christ, maybe no one will notice and it will all go away on its own. But it doesn't. It just gets a firmer hold and a longer reach, making it harder and harder for the Light to seep through an opening. Is it any wonder children are afraid of the dark? There may not be monsters under the bed, but they know innately that darkness is where demons hide.

Meditation: Have you ever been in a totally darkened room, maybe drifting off to sleep, when someone turns on a bright overhead light? It makes you recoil, hide your face, perhaps snap in anger. While that's a normal reaction for someone woken abruptly from sleep, it's also the way our interior selves tend to react to light shone on our faults and sins. We recoil, pull tight the curtain of our soul, turn our backs, but it's a lost cause. Light always finds a way in. Why not flick the switch yourself and put it all before God?

Prayer: Christ our Light, give me the courage to lay bare the sins I hide in the darkness, to seek forgiveness, to reconcile myself to you in the glorious light of your love.

Changing Dynamic

Readings: Acts 5:27-33; John 3:31-36

Scripture:
"We must obey God rather than men." (Acts 5:29b)

Reflection: No fear. That's all I can think when I read that fierce and unwavering statement from Peter in the face of opposition and threats from the Sanhedrin, knowing full well that he and the other apostles could be crucified just as Jesus was for talking back, for continuing to teach, for believing in the One their leaders thought they had destroyed. These men who were once full of fear are now so full of faith that they cannot even stop to worry about all the "What ifs," the consequences of their actions. They must obey God; there is no other option. It's the kind of faith I long for, the kind of faith I always think I'm inching toward and then something difficult comes along, a challenge that's a little too much for my weak spirit to take, and I fold like a house of cards. I feel like the girl in Flannery O'Connor's "A Temple of the Holy Ghost": "She could never be a saint, but she thought she could be a martyr if they killed her quick." I'm ready to follow as long as things aren't going to get too complicated, but, as we know, with the spiritual life it almost *always* gets complicated. Ours is not a faith for the faint of heart.

Peter and the others were fueled by something bigger and deeper than themselves, fueled by faith, yes, but more than that, by abiding trust. All doubt was gone. There would be no more denying. The resurrection changed everything, as it should for us. When we begin to waver, we can look back to this scene, Peter's clarity and courage, and we can pray for a taste of that.

Meditation: Put yourself in today's first reading alongside Peter. Or perhaps you're on the other side, one of the Sanhedrin in this scene. What is running through your mind as this conversation plays out? Do you feel fear or power? Is there any part of you that wants to run? How does this moment change the dynamic, change your life? What happens after this conversation ends that day, as the fury mounts among the Sanhedrin? Tap into this moment whenever the doubts start to creep in.

Prayer: Be not afraid, you tell us again and again. And we want so much to throw off fear and be brave in your name. Give us strength, Jesus, to be a rock like Peter.

Seeds of Faith

Readings: Acts 5:34-42; John 6:1-15

Scripture:
"For if this endeavor or this activity is of human origin, it will destroy itself. But if it comes from God, you will not be able to destroy them." (Acts 5:38b-39a)

Reflection: Fads and fame come and go; celebrities and all stars eventually lose the spotlight, no matter how great or how popular they once were. Nothing lasts forever. Or does it? What Jesus began could not be snuffed out by intimidation, threats, even death. In fact, those things only made Jesus' followers grow in number and strength.

"There is in fact in our midst Someone who is stronger than evil, stronger than the mafia, than the obscure conspiracies of those who profit at the expense of desperate people, than those who crush others with disdain," Pope Francis said during a weekly audience on June 28, 2017. "Christians therefore, must always be found on the "opposite side" of the world, that chosen by God: not persecutors but persecuted; not arrogant but meek; not charlatans but submissive to the truth; not imposters but honest men and women."

You would think with those kinds of requirements, this would not be a club anyone would want to join, and yet here we are. As we saw in today's first reading, many thought

Jesus would be another passing fad, his followers scattered in his absence. Except he was never absent, and he is not absent to us today. Even now, people are willing to die for that truth, for that Someone, for the endeavor that could not be destroyed.

Meditation: Pope Francis talks about Jesus as "Someone who is stronger than evil." Do you believe that? Do you believe Jesus is stronger than the rampant evil we see around us in the headlines every day? What challenges do you face as you try to conform your life to Jesus' teachings? Are you in the world or *of* the world? It's not easy to stay on the spiritual side of the world when the secular side has so much power and prestige. It's hard to give up glory for a backseat, but that's what Jesus did and what he asks of us. He ate with prostitutes and tax collectors, washed the feet of his disciples, moved along the margins of his society and was derided for it. Are we willing to do the same?

Prayer: Son of Justice, the signs of our times often point in the wrong direction. Help us to see clearly the path you have set out for us. As you taught us to pray, "Lead us not into temptation but deliver us from evil."

On Lion's Wings

Readings: 1 Pet 5:5b-14; Mark 16:15-20

Scripture:
Be sober and vigilant. Your opponent the Devil is prowling around like a roaring lion looking for someone to devour. Resist him. (1 Pet 5:8-9a)

Reflection: You can feel the push and pull of faith in today's readings, which give us both ends of the spectrum of this spiritual life. On the one hand, we hear Peter telling us to be on our guard because the devil is never far away, always looking for our weak spot. And then there is the Gospel of St. Mark, whose feast we celebrate today, reminding us that those who believe will be capable of doing amazing things in Jesus' name, although I wouldn't recommend picking up any serpents or drinking anything deadly no matter how far you manage to get on this spiritual path. Still, we get the point. With Jesus, we can do anything; without Jesus, we are easy prey to the lion who lies in wait.

How fitting that we have this image of the devil as a lion on the prowl as we celebrate the feast of St. Mark, whose symbol is a winged lion. One bound to what is below; one capable of reaching heaven, of escaping any traps the devil may set. Certainly St. Mark did that in his lifetime, as he set out to spread the Good News far from home and died a martyr's death. As always, Scripture grounds us in truth, calling us to remain "steadfast in faith, knowing that your brothers and sisters throughout the world undergo the same sufferings" (1 Pet 5:9b). True now as it was then.

Meditation: We don't typically think of the devil as a lion. Although it can be vicious, that creature seems too noble to be associated with the devil. We think of Aslan in C.S. Lewis's Narnia, or the not-really-cowardly lion of Frank L. Baum's Oz. Perhaps that is the cunning of the devil, taking a form that purports to be noble and using it for ill. If we're not paying attention, we might be tricked. Have there been times in your life when you truly believed something was good and true, only to find out later that it was a lie? Today let us give our lion wings so that rather than pounce on us when we are down, he will lift us above the fray and lead us to safety.

Prayer: Good St. Mark, pray for us as we face the darkness in our midst, the lions that hunt rather than the lions that soar. Give us wings to fly toward heaven.

Leave a Light On

Readings: Acts 2:14, 22-33; 1 Pet 1:17-21; Luke 24:13-35

Scripture:
But they urged him, "Stay with us, for it is nearly evening and the day is almost over." So he went in to stay with them. (Luke 24:29)

Reflection: Today we find ourselves again on the road to Emmaus, walking along with Cleopas and his companion. We sense their confusion and fear as they talk about the stories they're hearing, stories of a dead man raised, their crucified teacher talking to some of the women. They might have thought this was a trick of the devil or an outright fantasy. Imagine, then, when a stranger joins them and seems to say all the right things. They're not quite sure they understand, but one thing they know: They feel comfort when they are with him, less afraid. How good it would be to have this stranger alongside them as they face who-knows-what in the nights and days ahead.

Don't we often feel the same way about God? We catch a glimpse of God present in our lives, a sudden sense of peace, a feeling deep in our core that all is right with the world when previously it felt all wrong. We want to capture it, bottle it, beg God to stay right there. "Don't move!" we want to shout, so glad are we for this moment of comfort, this reminder that we are not alone. Of course, the moment usually passes, although we are the ones who move away from God rather than it being the other way around. God asks us if we will stay with him, not just for one day or night but forever. Stay. Don't move. God is right where you are right now.

Meditation: Have you ever been all alone in a strange place that should be filled with people? It can be unnerving. I've found myself on many occasions in empty retreat houses, where I am the only guest clanking around long hallways. I make my way to the chapel, hungry for the light above the tabernacle reminding me that I am not alone. In Jesus' presence I find comfort and safety, and I carry that feeling back to my lonely end of the hall. We can carry that with us always; we just tend to forget. Find a time this week to sit before a tabernacle and draw strength from the silent but powerful presence of God in the Blessed Sacrament.

Prayer: Jesus, you are the Bread of Life, the food that nourishes, the presence that comforts, the truth that lights the way. Stay with us; live in us.

Revisiting Lent

Readings: Acts 6:8-15; John 6:22-29

Scripture:
"Do not work for food that perishes but for the food that endures for eternal life, which the Son of Man will give you." (John 6:27)

Reflection: We all have to work for food that perishes, so today's Gospel can be a little unsettling to those of us bringing home a paycheck to keep the pantry full and the lights on. But there's a difference between working to live and living to work, and I think that may be at the heart of Jesus' message today: Do we put our faith in the earthly things we can buy? Have we made an idol of our job, our car, our specialty foods that can be bought only in certain stores? Or do we understand that those things are nice, but they are not important?

I was heading to a retreat house recently to spend two days in solitude and silence. I packed up a cooler bag with all my meals so I would not have to break the quietude of the hermit suite I'd been assigned. I was about forty-five minutes into my drive when I realized I left that cooler bag by the garage door. I had no food, and there would be no meals available. At first, I erupted in frustration, cursing my stupidity. But then God knocked some sense into me. This could be an opportunity. I could make due with whatever was available and live like a true hermit rather than a well-fed suburbanite. I ate a stale granola bar for lunch and popcorn for dinner. I found some dry cereal in the retreat center kitchen and a packet of peanut butter. My stomach growled now and then, but I was full on a deeper level, on a level that could not perish even if my cooler did.

Meditation: Take a look at how you spend your time, your money, your energy. Can you let some of the "perishables" drop away—maybe too much time on social media, too much money spent on clothes, too much energy spent on gaining prestige. Although we tend to think of fasting as something reserved for Lent, there is benefit to it any time of year. During this Easter season, can you revisit your Lenten promises and see if they could prove to be lifegiving even now?

Prayer: God of all creation, you have filled this world with beauty and wonder that we too often ignore and neglect. Give us eyes to see what is life-giving and a heart that chooses wisely.

On a Wing and a Prayer

Readings: Acts 7:51–8:1a; John 6:30-35

Scripture:
"You stiff-necked people, uncircumcised in heart and ears, you always oppose the Holy Spirit; you are just like your ancestors." (Acts 7:51)

Reflection: "Stiff-necked people." That terms stirs up quite an image, doesn't it? One that feels a little too close for comfort, at least from where I'm standing. I'm not typically stiff-necked, but sometimes that urge pushes its way into my spiritual life. Some challenge or disappointment shows up in my life, and I decide I will punish God by locking him out, blocking the Holy Spirit. Of course, obeying the Holy Spirit doesn't mean we have to be a doormat; often just the opposite. I think of some of our great saints, who were often anything but quiet in their determination to do the work of the Spirit. We just have to be sure we're on the right side.

I was watching the film *Vision*, about the life of the twelfth-century mystic St. Hildegard of Bingen, and I couldn't help but marvel at her absolute *chutzpah* in confronting abbots and bishops and even the pope. She got the job done, and often was disliked for it, but always she did what the Spirit asked. "Thus am I, a feather on the breath of God," she wrote. Feathers, so weightless and fragile, and yet, so captivating and free. When we allow the Spirit to carry us, we, too, become free, even when people disagree with us or oppose us with their stiff necks.

Meditation: Although we can picture it in our mind's eye, we rarely get to see a feather floating along on a breeze. Still there are similar things that evoke that same feeling: a leaf swirling from a tree top, a helium balloon flying up into the clouds. What do those images evoke for you? Do you enjoy the idea of floating freely without a set course, or do you like the solidity of being grounded or at least tethered? I was once in a marriage workshop where the facilitator asked if we'd rather be a kite or a clothesline. Neither answer was wrong, but one stays put and the other bounces around at the whim of the wind. Which are you? A feather, a leaf, a balloon, a clothesline, a kite? Ask the Spirit and then let the Spirit show you how to be the best version of you.

Prayer: Holy Spirit, we know that trusting you means letting go of our need to control things, floating rather than steering. Give us the grace to loosen our grip and let you lead the way.

April 29: Saint Catherine of Siena,
Virgin and Doctor of the Church

The Courage of Catherine

Readings: Acts 8:1b-8; John 6:35-40

Scripture:
"For this is the will of my Father, that everyone who sees the Son and believes in him may have eternal life, and I shall raise him on the last day." (John 6:40)

Reflection: Hanging in my office over my desk is an icon of St. Catherine of Siena. In this particular image, she has a large wooden ship—the Barque of Peter, representing the church—hoisted on her shoulder. Catherine is listing but strong under the weight of it. I hung it there to remind me that the church has been beset with problems and scandals and challenges in the past, and it takes every one of us to carry her forward. In her day, Catherine of Siena was involved not only in spiritual matters but in political ones and is credited with getting the pope to move the Holy See from Avignon back to Rome, no small feat. Catherine suffered for her faith but was undeterred. We can look to her when we feel ourselves listing, verging on capsizing, and remember that all is not lost, all is never lost, when we stay focused on Jesus.

"Start being brave about everything," St. Catherine wrote. "Drive out darkness and spread light. Don't look at your weaknesses. Realize instead that in Christ crucified you can do everything."

The earliest Christian community in today's first reading knew that firsthand. As they were dragged from their homes and imprisoned by Saul for their belief in Jesus Christ, they did not waver, because they knew the truth, because they believed in the eternal life that Jesus promises us again today.

Meditation: Bravery often feels like something someone else should do. The job of a superhero or a firefighter or a soldier. We often don't consider bravery something we need to fit onto our daily To Do list. Today's readings and feast day remind us that we are wrong on that count. Bravery is a daily decision. Maybe bravery is not responding in kind when someone mistreats us. Maybe bravery is going out of our comfort zone to help someone in trouble. Maybe bravery is making the parenting decisions our children need rather than the decisions they'd like. Chances are this day will present you with an opportunity to be brave. Take notice of it, and ask Jesus to give you the courage of Catherine.

Prayer: St. Catherine of Siena, you trusted in Jesus completely, even when it meant suffering, even when you had to do difficult things with bravery. Pray that we may find that same trust and strength as we face the challenges of our day.

A Beautiful Parade

Readings: Acts 8:26-40; John 6:44-51

Scripture:
"I am the living bread that came down from heaven; whoever eats this bread will live forever; and the bread that I will give is my flesh for the life of the world." (John 6:51)

Reflection: Sometimes when I'm at Mass and should have my head bowed in prayer after receiving Communion, I find myself looking instead at the line of people filing past me. And while that may not seem to be the most appropriate use of my post-Communion meditation time, it's precisely the thing that draws me deeper into communion with those around me. I see families juggling babies and toddlers, remembering my own earlier years of trying to figure out how to receive reverently while a child or two are tugging at my arm. Older couples, sleepy looking teens, freshly minted first communicants. It's a beautiful parade. A ragtag bunch sometimes, but so were the apostles. We're in good company. And with each person that files past, I feel love growing. We are in this together, all of us trying our best, which may not be good enough in our own minds but is probably more than good enough for God.

In a homily on the Body of Christ, Trappist Father Thomas Keating says that Christ physically present in the Eucharist on the altar at Mass "brings Christ close to us—closer than he was to his disciples on the roads of Jerusalem or in Galilee" and that it "binds the assembly into one."

I think it's easy to take the Eucharist for granted, so blessed are we to receive with regularity. But if ever you've been forced to be away from Communion for an extended time, you probably began to feel the pull toward home, toward Christ. Our bodies know what our souls need.

Meditation: The next time you go to Mass, use your post-Communion prayer time as an opportunity to pray for your parish community. As each person passes you, bless them silently and recognize your common bond in Jesus broken for us on the altar each day. Can you seek out the experience of another famous Trappist monk, Thomas Merton, who once stood on a street corner and felt uncontainable love for the people all around him? They were "shining like the sun," he said. See if you can catch a glimpse of that from your own parish pew.

Prayer: Lamb of God, we are not worthy of the gift of the Eucharist, but we are grateful for this spiritual food that draws us to you and to one another. May the Bread of Life transform us from the inside out.

May 1: Friday of the Third Week of Easter
(Saint Joseph the Worker)

God's Work

Readings: Acts 9:1-20; John 6:52-59, or, for the Memorial, Gen 1:26–2:3 or Col 3:14-15, 17, 23-24; Matt 13:54-58

Scripture:
"Is he not the carpenter's son?" Matt 13:55

Reflection: It's funny—and somehow fitting—that on this memorial of St. Joseph the Worker, a day to recognize one of our greatest saints, we have a Gospel reading that, in effect, disparages him and the work he did. When the crowds question Jesus' authority and ability to speak with such wisdom, they point to his immediate and obvious lineage: the son of the carpenter. How can Joseph's son do such things? Why isn't he working with wood as he was trained to do? To the people who knew him, Joseph was a laborer. He may have been a good one, but a carpenter and a prophet were lifetimes apart in Nazareth at that time, and maybe in our minds today. We think we can gauge someone by the work they do, but the truth is we are all so much more than things we do to earn a living. Joseph was no different.

Joseph the carpenter was as strong and sturdy and reliable as the furniture he likely built. When others might have cowered or run away or sought vengeance, he listened and acted righteously and protected. We don't see much of him in

Scripture, but every scene he's in, every clue tells us he was a good man, a man who put his family above everything except God, a man whose silent strength helped our salvation story come to its fruition. Without Joseph the carpenter, our redemption hangs in the balance.

Meditation: Joseph would have taught Jesus everything he knew about being a carpenter. Jesus, no doubt, was a carpenter as well. For those many hidden years in Scripture, we can imagine that Jesus is working alongside Joseph, sawing, carving, nailing, sanding. But, no doubt, so much more was being taught in that workshop. Patience and strength, determination and perseverance. Think about your own work. Beyond the obvious, what does it teach you about life? What might you learn from your work, your workplace, your colleagues? Perhaps there is much more there than what meets the eye. As you go about your work today, even if your work is at home or in retirement or in school, notice the deeper lessons waiting for you there.

Prayer: St. Joseph, give us the quiet strength to do the work we are called to do without complaint. We look to you as our role model as we seek out the deeper meaning of our daily tasks.

May 2: Saint Athanasius,
Bishop and Doctor of the Church

All In

Readings: Acts 9:31-42; John 6:60-69

Scripture:
Many of the disciples of Jesus who were listening said, "This saying is hard; who can accept it?" (John 6:60)

Reflection: So many of the things Jesus taught were hard for followers to accept, but perhaps none more than the teaching on the Eucharist. The changing of bread and wine to body and blood, broken and shared, was beyond anything they could—or wanted to—comprehend. In many ways, it was not only confusing but abhorrent to them, so much so that we're told many left the fold. And Jesus, knowing full well that even his most dedicated disciples might have been planning a similar getaway, asks bluntly, "Are you leaving too?"

I often think Jesus is probably posing that question to me at least once a day, what with my difficulty in accepting what the Gospel requires me to do. "This saying is hard," I say, maybe not in so many words but in the things, big and small, that make up my daily life—the important things that get short shrift because I'm obsessing too much over the superficial stuff, the skirmishes and stresses, the hurts and offenses, the carelessness and inattentiveness to the many gifts that make up my living and breathing, even the not-so-great moments, which are gifts of their own. Just when I think I'm too wounded to walk back the pain, beyond the healing that comes from Eucharist and sacrament, something nudges me, and, like Peter, I find myself thinking, "If not Jesus, then who? If not here, then where?"

Meditation: Venerable Dorothy Day, founder of the Catholic Worker movement, quoting her longtime spiritual director Father John J. Hugo, often said, "I really only love God as much as I love the person I love the least." Talk about a saying that's hard. That's the first thing I thought of when I heard today's Gospel. We think we love God enough, but when we reflect on Dorothy's words, we get a glimpse of how far we have to go and how, when we don't love God fully, it's easier to walk away when things get hard. Who is it in your life that you love the least? Pray for that person today. Love that person. Don't make a show of it. Keep this one between you and God, and see what happens when you turn toward the hard sayings instead of walking away.

Prayer: God of understanding, you know the temptations of human weakness. Keep us steadfast when we want to run; help us love when we want to hate.

Gate Change

Readings: Acts 2:14a, 36-41; 1 Pet 2:20b-25; John 10:1-10

Scripture:
He testified with many other arguments, and was exhorting them, "Save yourselves from this corrupt generation." (Acts 2:40)

Reflection: We humans tend to be pretty self-centered. I'm sure many of us look around and think we are living in the most corrupt generation, the most troubled world, the most difficult times. When we hear Peter's words in the first reading today, we're reminded that the more things change, the more they stay the same, and, sadly, history really does repeat itself. We are not unique after all, afflicted as we are with our shared human frailty that causes us to turn against one another, to put self first, to seek ways around obstacles by stepping over or on someone else.

The Gospel reminds us of that fact, too, pointing out that if we attempt to climb over the gate rather than enter via the way of the shepherd, we are nothing more than thieves. The only way in is through—through Jesus Christ, the shepherd who calls us by name, whose voice we hear amid our confusion but don't always heed. We stray from the flock to find greener pastures on our own, thinking we can save ourselves. But we can't save ourselves, can we? We learned that on Good Friday and again on Easter morning and again every time we kneel before God in the Eucharist and remember that this is our gate, the entry point to our salvation, and the path that leads away from corruption and straight to the heart of God.

Meditation: Peter's words can be misleading if we take them out of context. "Save yourselves." But what's the rest of his admonition? Do we save ourselves by exercising more, eating right, donating to a worthy cause? No. "Repent and be baptized," he says, in order to be forgiven and to receive the Holy Spirit. So that's the good news of the Good News. We don't have to save ourselves; we can't save ourselves. All we can do is turn ourselves over to Jesus, fully and completely and let the healing power of his mercy and love go to work. What gate are you trying to climb over today? What would happen if you go through instead?

Prayer: Jesus, the Good Shepherd, call out to us when we are straying from the course you've set, lead us when we are lost. Even when we stand at the gate unwilling to enter, we pray that you will patiently wait for us to follow.

Open Invitation

Readings: Acts 11:1-18; John 10:11-18

Scripture:
"If then God gave them the same gift he gave to us when we came to believe in the Lord Jesus Christ, who was I to be able to hinder God?" (Acts 11:17)

Reflection: In our divided and divisive world, even we Christians can get caught up in the judgment game, blaming others and claiming victory for ourselves. This holier-than-thou attitude isn't restricted to one viewpoint or side; it's an equal opportunity offender. It's really the devil at work. When followers of Jesus are divided among themselves, it leaves room for evil to seep, or, at the very least, for chasms of disagreement to widen. We fight with each other and, in the process, the people "out there" look at us and wonder why anyone would want to join.

As Peter makes a case for the Gentiles in today's first reading, we see the first inklings of this in our earliest spiritual forebears. Like us, they wanted it to be a closed group, only for those who met certain criteria—their criteria. Author Anne Lamott once famously wrote, "You can safely assume you've created God in your own image when it turns out God hates all the same people you do." Ouch. The truth hurts. So often we try to "hinder" God, refusing to allow or accept that all can be saved, all are invited. We don't get to RSVP for anyone but ourselves. We can extend invitations and dress in our best outfits, but this is not some club with a velvet rope and a buff bouncer. Come as you are, even if you are broken and bedraggled.

Meditation: I think every child at some point secretly wants to be part of the "in" crowd at school. There is something intoxicating about being in an elite group, being chosen. But who deems the cool kids cool? Usually they create the storyline and the rest of us are foolish enough to buy into it. Our faith turns the in crowd on its head, telling us the last will be first. So why are we still caught up in the notion of limiting the possibilities? Control. We hate to give up control, but, if we do, if we fall back into God as though "hopelessly defeated," we will, in the words of *The Cloud of Unknowing*, feel as though we are "melting in water." Experience what it feels like to melt into God today.

Prayer: God of all, we pray today for unity, to see clearly our common humanity, our shared gift of salvation. Open our hearts to all that is possible when we get out of our own way.

Q & A

Readings: Acts 11:19-26; John 10:22-30

Scripture:
"How long are you going to keep us in suspense? If you are the Christ, tell us plainly." (John 10:24)

Reflection: Be careful what you wish for. How often do we pray for something, only to get it and find ourselves flummoxed and flustered, angry and outraged? It was not what we thought it would be. Bait and switch, we cry. I imagine that when I read today's Gospel, where the crowd first asks Jesus to "plainly" tell them whether he is the Messiah. After a pretty powerful and poetic message, he gives them what they want: "The Father and I are one." We don't get to see what happens next in today's particular reading, but it continues like this: "The Jews picked up rocks to stone him" (John 10:31). What did they think a Messiah might say? Was there anything the Messiah could say without causing outrage? Not likely.

Jesus walks through his world curing the sick, healing the lame, giving sight to the blind, and still he is asked, Are you the One? Signs and symbols don't convince them. Even Jesus' own words don't convince them. Even the cross won't convince them. But resurrection? That's a different story. We bask in the Easter season knowing that our God suffered and died for us but then rose again, giving answer to the question that haunted his followers. We are no longer kept in suspense. We know the truth, and the truth has set us free.

Meditation: It would be nice if we could have all our questions answered plainly—about the job offer, the diagnosis, the cross-country move. We can make ourselves sick with worry, as if the knot in our stomach is somehow holding all the loose ends of our life together. Without our worrying, wouldn't it all unravel and be lost? Our faith gives us the paradox: only when we stop holding on so tight will we finally have all that we want. It's not an easy ask. And so often when we do finally get our answer it's the opposite of what we wanted to hear. We'd like to throw something or scream, and sometimes we do scream—to God, at God. That's okay. Because God just keeps coming back, trying to give us a version of an answer that we'll finally be willing to hear.

Prayer: Speak to us, Lord, even when we refuse to listen. Speak to us in the quiet of our hearts where your voice brings peace and rest to our weary souls.

May 6: Wednesday of the Fourth Week of Easter

Imperfect Offering

Readings: Acts 12:24–13:5a; John 12:44-50

Scripture:
"I came into the world as light, so that everyone who believes in me might not remain in darkness." (John 12:46)

Reflection: At this time of year, we are blessed with an abundance of light. The days feel like they are longer as we march toward summer, and sunset seems to wait until the last possible minute. The sun forces new life up from the earth; the stars glimmer in the clear night sky as we sit by the flickering light of a campfire. It's like a symphony of light that buoys our spirits and allows us to shake off the doldrums that took hold over the long winter months. Light has a way of changing everything, and it manages to find its way in any way it can—through clouds and cracks, between leaves and sometimes even between raindrops. Light always finds a way.

Jesus reminds us today that he is that light, coming into the world to pull us out of the darkness we tend toward when left to our own devices and to shine his hope and mercy into the recesses where we keep the things that tie us down to fear and despair and anger and jealousy. Jesus doesn't just shine a light; he is the light. Like the sun that rises and sets on our days, Jesus is the light around which we revolve. If we are lucky and if we follow where his light leads, we may get the chance to reflect that light onto the darkness we find in the world, like the moon that illuminates a night sky through no power of its own.

Meditation: In the well-known Leonard Cohen song "Anthem," he sings, "Ring them bells that still can ring. Forget your perfect offering. There is a crack, a crack in everything. That's how the light gets in." Think about the way a kaleidoscope works, with the light hitting the broken shards of colored glass as they spin in a tube. Taken as single slivers, they might not be that spectacular, but together with the light filtering through they become a work of art, a joy to behold. Look at the kaleidoscope that is your life right now. If you turn toward the Light and let it filter through all your sharp edges and broken parts, you will see the work of art that you, too, are.

Prayer: Light of the World, illuminate the darkest corners of our hearts so that we may be reflections of your love and help to light the way for others.

Spiritual Disruption

Readings: Acts 13:13-25; John 13:16-20

Scripture:
"From now on I am telling you before it happens, so that when it happens you may believe that I AM." (John 13:19)

Reflection: We tend to like to compartmentalize God, as we compartmentalize so much of our lives. We like to put things into neat little boxes, the Divine included. God here. Jesus there. Holy Spirit always in the most unexpected places. Today, as Jesus speaks with the apostles, he uses words he knows will convey unity with the Father: I AM. No compartments here. The ancient words as spoken to Moses from the burning bush. Two tiny, simple words that convey mystery beyond anything we can hope to fully grasp here on earth. I AM.

Each time we make the Sign of the Cross and utter words so familiar they rush from our mouths like the air we breathe, we profess our belief in I AM, the triune God, who is and was and is to come, but I think too often we let that truth slip beneath the surface of our spiritual lives. We can easily fall into the secular world's way of seeing Jesus—a great spiritual teacher—and leave him in that compartment, apart from God. Jesus tell us he and the Father are one and that if we believe in him, we believe in the One who sent him. How often do we take the time to reflect on that incredibly deep truth that is only comprehensible with the eyes and heart of faith? We don't come to this understanding through books or lectures; we come to it through whatever figurative burning bush ignites the fire of God's love in our lives. Look for the sparks.

Meditation: If you're of a certain age, you may remember making the Sign of the Cross (or seeing your parent or grandparent do so) any time you drove past a church or heard a siren. Similarly, you may have been taught to bow your head slightly every time you said the word Jesus. Although those practices have gone out of fashion, small gestures that disrupt our non-stop motion for even the briefest moment can be helpful to our spiritual lives. Although I probably learned it when I was only seven years old, bowing my head at Jesus' name will still give me pause. What small practice can you put in place this week to call yourself back to God now and then?

Prayer: Tell us so we may believe. Show us so we may follow. Father, Son, and Spirit, guide us ever homeward.

Altered Reality

Readings: Acts 13:26-33; John 14:1-6

Scripture:
"Do not let your hearts be troubled." (John 14:1)

Reflection: We live in troubled times, so it's really no surprise that we often find our hearts troubled. For some of us the trouble is right now, right here—an illness, a job loss, a marriage failing, a child in crisis. For others of us the trouble is in all the "What ifs." Whether we're looking ahead to starting a family or looking ahead to retirement, there are troubles that work their way into our minds even when they have not yet worked their way into our realities. In today's Gospel, Jesus tells his followers not to worry. If they have faith in him, they already know how to get to where they need to go. And Thomas says what all the others were probably thinking: No, we don't.

How often do we say we don't know how we're going to get through a busy week, a busy season, a rough patch of life? It threatens to overwhelm, the uncertainty of it all. Like the disciples, we wonder how we'll do it. Yes, we have faith in God but that's not going to pay the bills or get the next big work project done. Or is it? When we learn not to be troubled and to trust in God, we find that the problems may still be there, but they feel less burdensome, because we recognize that, ultimately, nothing on this earth can derail our joy and our faith without our consent.

Meditation: In *New Seeds of Contemplation*, famed Trappist monk Thomas Merton wrote, "No despair of ours can alter the reality of things, or stain the joy of the cosmic dance which is always there." Do you sometimes imagine that your despair or worry can alter your situation? Awake at night, staring into the darkness, we spin our wheels thinking that all that energy spent on worry is actually getting things done, but it's doing just the opposite—wearing us out and making us less likely to be ready for whatever is ahead. Same in our spiritual life. Stop the spinning and worrying and pour all of that energy into prayer and joy and life with God and in service to others. Suddenly worry gives way to dancing, even if only on the inside.

Prayer: Although I am often troubled, I trust in you, Jesus. Lead me to the dwelling place where there is no need to fear.

Dark Joy

Readings: Acts 13:44-52; John 14:7-14

Scripture:
The disciples were filled with joy and the Holy Spirit. (Acts 13:52)

Reflection: When we catch up with the disciples in the first reading today, there is seemingly no reason for them to be joyful, at least not by human standards. There are threats of violence; persecution is being stirred up; they are expelled from the city. We might expect the next line in that Scripture verse to tell us that they left in shame, heads hanging. I'm guessing that's how I would have felt had I been in their place. But instead they are filled with joy, because they know that what they are doing—and what is being done to them because of it—is bigger than everything. For those of us who've never come close to that kind of Spirit moment in our lives, there may be a pang of jealousy or at least curiosity. What is it like to feel that way, so sure of our calling and our mission and our God that nothing, not even threats of death, can steal our joy?

Part of the problem stems from our society's view of happiness and joy. There's a danger in thinking they're the same; people of faith know that happiness is fine but fleeting. Inevitably, something comes along that makes us sad or mad.

But joy? That's a different story. Joy comes from deep within and can't be shaken by bad weather or traffic jams, even illness or work issues. Because joy is grounded in God, and God is never fleeting.

Meditation: When was the last time you felt joy in spite of less-than-perfect outward circumstances? When it happens, I bet you notice, because it's a gift. You may have every reason to scream but something inside—Spirit whispering, perhaps—says, "It's okay. This is not going to break you." And you stand up, shake the dust off your feet, and say, "Bring it." I'll admit that I long for that kind of deep-seated, unshakeable joy. It doesn't come easily to me, but I know it when I see it and I revel in it when I get a taste. The next time something happens that typically gets you frustrated, take a cue from the disciples instead.

Prayer: God of joy, you fill our lives with blessings that so often go unnoticed. Give us the grace to be joyful in both our abundance and lack and to recognize that you are present in all.

Sacred Stones

Readings: Acts 6:1-7; 1 Pet 2:4-9; John 14:1-12

Scripture:
Like living stones, let yourselves be built into a spiritual house. (1 Pet 2:5)

Reflection: My husband and I went on a hike through a nearby nature preserve recently, and as we made our way down the rough path through the woods, we came upon the remnants of an old stone house, crumbling but beautiful and very much alive despite its dilapidated state. There's something about old stones that make them special, sacred. It's as though they're breathing history into our lungs, reminding us to protect and preserve our own sacred places lest they weaken and fall down. Moss-covered, marked with fossils or maybe even carved initials or dates, they speak to us from the distant past with both warning and hope.

If you were to take some large rocks and put them one on top of the other, you'd likely end up with a haphazard pile rather than a meandering wall or sturdy shelter. You need a stoneworker, a master builder to guide the process. God asks us to do the same in our spiritual lives—let Jesus guide our spiritual building so that our living stones work together to create something far beyond the sum of its parts. With Jesus, we can build a spiritual home, a sacred space within that will never crumble because it is centered on and supported by the Cornerstone that is our Savior.

Meditation: Take notice of the stones and rocks that make up the physical landscape of your life. Perhaps there's a low wall in your garden or a stone firepit or fireplace. Maybe you collect pebbles and stones from places you visit. As you drive about your region, notice boulders that have been cut through to make way for a road or rocks piled high or perhaps carefully arranged. Now look at the spiritual stones that make up your life. What kind of configuration do you have, and where is Jesus in the mix? Is Jesus the bedrock that serves as the base for everything else, or is Jesus the stone on the edge, maybe hidden under a pile of larger rocks that block you from his light and love? What would it take to lift those obstacles away to reveal the living stones of your life?

Prayer: Lord, you are my rock, my salvation, the foundation upon which I want to build my life, my future. Make my daily actions, words, and thoughts living stones that build up rather than tear down.

Castle Walls

Readings: Acts 14:5-18; John 14:21-26

Scripture:
"Whoever loves me will keep my word, and my Father will love him, and we will come to him and make our dwelling with him." (John 14:23)

Reflection: In her book *Interior Castle*, St. Teresa of Avila writes about God dwelling within us in poetic prose that gets to the heart of the main thing that often gets in our way:

> As to what good qualities there may be in our souls, or Who dwells within them, or how precious they are—those are things which we seldom consider and so we trouble little about carefully preserving the soul's beauty. All our interest is centered in the rough setting of the diamond, and in the outer wall of the castle—that is to say, in these bodies of ours.

It doesn't matter that this Doctor of the Church wrote those words more than four hundred years ago. It turns out that human beings are similar at our core no matter what the era. We look at ourselves in the mirror and see our imperfections; we can't imagine God dwelling within us because, quite frankly, we're having a difficult enough time dwelling there ourselves. But St. Teresa reminds us that our physical selves are merely the outer wall of this castle with many rooms, the place where God resides. Can we learn to look past our outer wall and seek out the One speaking to us from deep within the center room of our heart? Can we, as Jesus challenges in today's Gospel, keep his word so that Father, Son, and Spirit will find a welcome place in us?

Meditation: When you invite people to your house, you probably spend a fair amount of time getting ready—cooking, cleaning, maybe even doing some of those chores that rarely get done, washing windows or decluttering closets. Candles glow, music plays, and the smell of food wafts out the door when we open it. What's the spiritual equivalent? What do we need to do to ready our interior castle for the most important visitor we could possibly entertain? It's not all that unlike the house prep. We need to declutter our minds, create an open space inside, clear out the things that get in the way of our relationship with God. Light a candle, put on some peaceful music, and open the door to the One who is waiting to be invited in.

Prayer: God of patience, thank you for bearing with my tendency to ignore you amid the busyness of my life. Today I begin to clear a bigger space for you. Come, Lord Jesus.

Promises, Promises

Readings: Acts 14:19-28; John 14:27-31a

Scripture:
"It is necessary for us to undergo many hardships to enter the Kingdom of God." (Acts 14:22b)

Reflection: Things are tough all over in today's readings. Violence and intimidation in the first reading as Paul is stoned and dragged from the city; in the Gospel, uncertainty and fear among the disciples as Jesus tells them he is going away. But in the midst of it all, hope and promises—promises of a kingdom that awaits us, promises of peace, promises of an Advocate who will stay with us always. Those same promises belong to us, but we, like those early disciples, often fall prey to the troubles that dog us. We forget that the day-to-day struggles that scare us are not the end game. They are not even a means to an end. They are just moments in an earthly life that is the tiniest fraction of our eternal life.

That's a challenge for most of us to grasp. Everything we do in this world seems monumental when it's happening to us, and some of it is pretty critical as a life goes—raising children, supporting a family, building a marriage. But when we put it in perspective, as Paul tries to do for us, we remember that we are not as important as we think we are. We will all have to suffer a bit; such is the nature of human life. But we do not suffer alone. We have a future, even when we no longer have breath, because we have an Advocate who leads us day by day toward the kingdom God has built for us. That promise trumps everything the world can throw at us.

Meditation: What trouble is weighing you down today? Is it an overwhelming worry about a child, bills that can't be paid, a diagnosis you're fearing? Can you give it to God for even one day? Sometimes the troubles that overwhelm us are things that shouldn't be given so much power: a difficult job, a full calendar, a house that needs cleaning. We turn those passing worries into mountains that block our path to God. It's easier to focus on the job or the house than it is to focus on what really matters—our eternal salvation. So, we busy ourselves with an endless list of "What ifs" rather than accept what *is* and live our lives accordingly.

Prayer: Eternal God, help us to see clearly the truly important things in our day-to-day lives and to find you in the midst of them.

May 13: Wednesday of the Fifth Week of Easter
(Our Lady of Fatima)

Necessary Pruning

Readings: Acts 15:1-6; John 15:1-8

Scripture:
"I am the true vine, and my Father is the vine grower." (John 15:1)

Reflection: This feast of Our Lady of Fatima, which has no Scriptural reference, seems perfectly tied to today's Gospel. The Spirit at work. The image of the branches either clinging to the vine or withering and ending up as kindling seems to echo the messages the three children received from Mary as they tended sheep in a village in Portugal more than a century ago: pray and do penance in order to save yourselves and the world.

Much focus over the years has been on the secrets of Fatima, but more than the prophetic messages, Fatima offered a way to God by amending our own lives and praying for others. It's another way of looking at the pruning process that is used to describe our spiritual lives in today's Gospel. Even the good branches must be pruned in order to produce more fruit. Although we may not like to admit it, we usually know where and what in our life could use some gentle pruning and shaping or, in some cases, maybe even the power of an axe or chainsaw. Life has a way of getting messy and dragging us along with it if we don't take time regularly to pray and reflect and make some hard sacrifices. If three little children in a field could grasp that, maybe we can do the same.

Meditation: Where does your life need pruning? What are you willing to sacrifice? Perhaps more importantly, what are you *not* willing to sacrifice? Start there, because that's probably the most likely thing that's getting in the way of your spiritual journey. Now add prayer, but not just any prayer. On this feast of Our Lady of Fatima, take out your rosary beads. I know you have them, probably multiple sets tucked away in all sorts of places—nightstand, office, pocket. Even if we don't tend to say the rosary with regularity, many of us keep the beads close by, a reminder of just how powerful this prayer is. Today, make time to say the rosary. If that seems daunting, start with just one decade. Let the rhythm of the prayers wash over you and give you the courage to do the pruning that needs to be done.

Prayer: O my Jesus, forgive us our sins, save us from the fire of hell. Lead all souls to heaven, especially those most in need of your mercy.

Winners and Losers

Readings: Acts 1:15-17, 20-26; John 15:9-17

Scripture:
So they proposed two, Joseph called Barsabbas, who was also known as Justus, and Matthias. (Acts 1:23)

Reflection: Losing is never easy, especially when it's out there in public for all to see. That's why, on this feast of St. Matthias, the apostle chosen to replace Judas Iscariot, it seems even more fitting to focus on the guy who lost: Justus. That's a pretty big seat to lose—not just a town board or city council but one of *the* Twelve. I would imagine that Justus had every reason to feel let down, angry, and resentful. Would anyone have blamed him if he said, "If I'm not good enough to be part of the inner circle, I don't want to be part of it at all." We'd nod our heads and think he showed them. But that's not what he did. According to history, he continued to proclaim the Good News and died a martyr's death. By the standards of our society, he was a loser in every category. Fortunately, God doesn't do things by the standards of society; just the opposite.

He takes the downtrodden, the beaten down, the miserable and makes them the ones who should be emulated and honored. Because they suffered for his sake. They did not put themselves above God, even when the cost was life itself, because life is not worth anything at all if living it requires us to cut ourselves off from God. The heroes of the early church knew they could lose everything on earth and gain the kingdom. Turns out there was no loser in today's first reading, even if we don't hear it that way.

Meditation: Has there ever been a time when you've lost out on an important position or award—a job you really wanted, an honor you thought you deserved, maybe even just a compliment or sign of appreciation from your boss. It hurts, and, often, it can make us want to go our own way in order to prove a point or make someone else suffer. Today's readings, from the vote for a new apostle to Jesus teaching that we must be willing to lay down our lives for a friend, are reminders that losing is often winning in God's eyes. The last shall be first, even when being last feels like the end of the world to us.

Prayer: Sts. Matthias and Justus, give us the courage to follow God's will, even when it is not easy. Show us the way to say yes to hard questions.

Difficult Love

Readings: Acts 15:22-31; John 15:12-17

Scripture:
"This I command you: love one another." (John 15:17)

Reflection: Jesus' challenge today is not only the greatest commandment, it's the toughest. It's easy to love God, but loving everyone else is a tall order when everyone else typically finds a way to push our buttons on a regular basis. Whether it's the nightly news or a coworker or the person in the car in front of us, we are easily pulled off course when it comes to this commandment. We tend to love those who love us or those who are suffering in some way and deserve our concern and compassion. And in those moments, we might think, "I've got this." And then, and then . . . the light turns green and the car stays put, the driver clearly looking at a cell phone. Love goes out the window, perhaps along with a few choice words.

C.S. Lewis of Narnia fame, in a chapter on charity in his book *Mere Christianity*, writes:

> Do not waste time bothering whether you 'love' your neighbor; act as if you did. As soon as we do this we find one of the great secrets. When you are behaving as if you loved someone, you will presently come to love him. If you injure

someone you dislike, you will find yourself disliking him more. If you do him a good turn, you will find yourself disliking him less.

That puts today's Gospel into practical terms, daunting but doable if we're willing. Are we willing?

Meditation: Couples who attend Marriage Encounter weekends are told to "make a decision to love" in order to build up their spousal relationships, but when I read that C.S. Lewis quote, I realized that suggestion applies to all of life. Make a decision to love—at home, at work, in the grocery store, on the ballfield. When we do so, even in the face of someone who is difficult to love or has done something to hurt us, we soften and begin to see the frailty that exists there under the hardened façade or seething silence. We are essentially all the same, but we forget. Today, make a decision to love, and see how it changes your interactions with everyone around you. How does it feel to love without getting love in return?

Prayer: God of unconditional love, we struggle to live up to your greatest commandment. Open our hearts to those who cross our paths so that we may love as you do.

Change Is Inevitable

Readings: Acts 16:1-10; John 15:18-21

Scripture:
Day after day the churches grew stronger in faith and increased in number. (Acts 16:5)

Reflection: It's easy to imagine that the early disciples somehow had less of a challenge with faith. After all, they were close to Jesus. Some knew him firsthand; others knew him through the apostles, or even through powerful visions that could knock them headlong off a horse. In today's first reading, we hear that the churches grew stronger day by day and think that if only we had their experiences, we, too, could grow our churches at a time when attendance and engagement seems to be going in the wrong direction. But follow the course of that reading down a little further and another line sets things straight: ". . . they tried to go on into Bithynia, but the Spirit of Jesus did not allow them."

Things were not as cut and dry as we might assume. Entire areas were blocked from even hearing the Good News for reasons we may not understand. But carry on they did, to a different region, where the reception might be welcoming. Are we as persistent, as unfazed by obstacles when it comes to speaking and living the Gospel, especially in a world that isn't particularly fond of its message? In today's Gospel,

Jesus tell us directly that we can expect the world to hate us because we "do not belong to the world." Our mission is not an easy one. What is the Spirit of Jesus asking of us? Are we listening?

Meditation: Think of your own parish church. Depending on where you live, your pews might be filled to overflowing. Give thanks for that blessing. If you are in other regions, where populations in general are declining or moving, your church might be sparsely populated or on the verge of closure. In cities where communities once thrived and every block seemed to be home to multiple ethnic parishes, doors are locked. Our church is a living, breathing Body of Christ. That means we move and change, decrease and expand. Like so many other aspects of our lives, nothing stays stagnant. Can we accept that and work with it, instead of against it? Can we hear the Spirit telling us when we need to go somewhere new, despite our strongest inclinations to stay put?

Prayer: Spirit of Jesus, speak to us as we discern what is ahead. Open our ears to your challenge and give us strength to move forward.

May 17: Sixth Sunday of Easter

Alone in the Crowd

Readings: Acts 8:5-8, 14-17; 1 Pet 3:15-18; John 14:15-21

Scripture:
"I will not leave you orphans; I will come to you." (John 14:18)

Reflection: We live in a world where loneliness is a growing epidemic. We are more connected than ever thanks to the internet and social media, and yet the very thing that connects us often causes us to become more isolated. In the glow of our screen, we sit alone and "talk" to "friends" out there. We may even be surrounded by family members or coworkers or a crowd on a train, but, at the same time, deep within our hearts we may feel very much alone, orphaned. It's clear from Jesus' words in today's Gospel that the fear of being alone isn't something reserved for the iPhone generation. Jesus' followers, though bound together by their common belief, know he's going away, and they are afraid. We get it. We're afraid too.

Like those early disciples, however, we have access to the very same graces they did; we have an Advocate. As Jesus promised then and now, we are not orphans. Jesus lives within us, the Spirit swirls around us, the Father watches over us. What a comforting reality. Now, you may say, "Well, yes, but I'm still alone in my house." If you let the Spirit do its work and if you respond to the Spirit's call, you won't be alone for long, because the Spirit grows in community. If we allow the Spirit to lead, we will soon find ourselves surrounded by others who, just like us, are hungry for a connection to God and to those who love God.

Meditation: When was the last time you put yourself out there and took a chance on introducing yourself to someone new, or joined a group or class that has always piqued your interest? Although we can count on God to be with us always, it's nice to have people who support us on the journey. This week, make an effort to look at your parish bulletin or community newspaper and find a new meeting or class or organization that could use your help or talents, or that you could learn from. Let the Spirit guide you. Or find one person who could use a friend, a ride, a meal, and be that connection for someone else.

Prayer: Spirit of God, although we know in our hearts you are with us, help us to become more aware of your presence in our lives and to bring that presence out into the world.

The Color Purple

Readings: Acts 16:11-15; John 15:26–16:4a

Scripture:
One of them, a woman named Lydia, a dealer in purple cloth, from the city of Thyatira, a worshiper of God, listened, and the Lord opened her heart to pay attention to what Paul was saying. (Acts 16:14)

Reflection: A dealer in purple cloth. What a gorgeous jewel of a detail given to us in today's first reading. As if the presence of Lydia isn't enough to make our spiritual heads spin, the added detail about her trade kicks everything up a notch and, if we've drifted off a bit, we're at full attention now. Who is this woman? Clearly someone of significance to the newly forming church to garner this kind of attention in the Acts of the Apostles and clearly someone of significance in her community to have had the ability to invite Paul and his fellow missionaries to stay in her home and to have her household be baptized en masse. How many Lydias were out there in the early church, risking comfort and safety for a faith being preached by men from afar? What was it that opened Lydia's heart to the message? Yes, the Spirit, but what words did Paul say, what moved her to go out on a limb? What would move us to do the same?

Ours is not a faith for the faint of heart. As we see in Scripture, not long after Lydia's conversion and kind gesture, Paul and Silas find themselves on the wrong side of an angry mob. The juxtaposition of the two scenes is jarring. In one, faith and hope wrapped up in a kind of mysticism shrouded in the majesty of purple; in the other, fear and greed expressed in the violence of beatings and jail cells. This is the story of our faith: hope in the face of suffering; trust in the face of fear; faith in the face of persecution.

Meditation: What if your faith story was given a spot in the New Testament? How would the writers describe you? What details of your life would make us pause and hunger for more? Today imagine yourself as a modern-day Lydia, visited by missionaries preaching in a way that moves you to reform your life and make a bigger space for God. What might you do? What would it take to give you the courage to take a leap and be Lydia to the church of today?

Prayer: Holy women of the early church, give us the courage to take risks for our faith, to put ourselves out there when we hear the truth, to bear witness to what Jesus taught with our lives.

A Spiritual Catch-22

Readings: Acts 16:22-34; John 16:5-11

Scripture:
"But I tell you the truth, it is better for you that I go. For if I do not go, the Advocate will not come to you." (John 16:7)

Reflection: We tend not to like goodbyes. Usually it hurts more than is comfortable and fills us with a little fear, whether we're the one going or the one left behind. In the case of a permanent separation, like death, saying goodbye can be unbearable. We cannot imagine life without our loved one. And yet, we know that goodbyes are necessary and, sometimes, beneficial. As difficult as it may be to say goodbye to a child leaving for college, we know that the leaving will result in a more independent and well-rounded child. Similarly, leaving a job, a home, even a friendship that has become untenable may cause anxiety and make us sad even as we recognize the good that will come from the decision.

The disciples in the Gospel today are facing one of those major goodbyes. I'm guessing it was the kind of separation that left them paralyzed with fear and sadness. But Jesus tells them that the goodbye will lead to better things. They cannot have the Spirit until they say goodbye to Jesus. A catch-22 if ever there was one. We don't ever have to face that decision when it comes to God. The Spirit is ours for the taking, if our hearts are open. Although we know that, ultimately, we will have to face the goodbye of a lifetime—our own—in order to get the reward of eternity. We can have it all, but it comes at a price.

Meditation: What goodbye in your life left you beyond consolation? It's likely that you can still conjure up exactly what you felt at that moment, right down to the smells in the room or the color of the sky outside. Moments like that leave a permanent scar. But now, maybe years later, despite the fact that you wish that goodbye never had to happen, can you see the places where the goodbye presented you with a gift of some sort? Maybe you have a closer relationship with a sibling or parent because of a mutual loss you suffered. Maybe you now have a wonderful work community because you were laid off from a previous job. Can you begin to look at the hard moments of your life and find the places where God poured grace into them?

Prayer: Spirit of God, be with us when we struggle, comfort us when we grieve, lead us to where grace is waiting.

Nearer Still

Readings: Acts 17:15, 22–18:1; John 16:12-15

Scripture:
"He made from one the whole human race to dwell on the entire surface of the earth, and he fixed the ordered seasons and the boundaries of their regions, so that people might seek God, even perhaps grope for him and find him, though indeed he is not far from any one of us." (Acts 17: 26-27)

Reflection: When was the last time you "groped" for God, desperately reaching out—perhaps literally—in the hope of grasping onto something, anything, that would convince you that God was not far away from you? To our ears, this groping might sound a little too desperate. If we're prayerful and holy enough, shouldn't we be able to find God in a more civilized manner? But in today's first reading we hear Paul tell us that God created everything—the heavens and seasons and all of us on this planet—so that we "might seek God, even perhaps grope for him and find him." In other words, God *wants* us to come after him, to reach him, to know him, to feel him nearby. Even though God is always nearby. What a fascinating and funny God we have! God wants us to actively make a connection; ours is not a passive faith.

In *The Practice of the Presence of God*, Brother Lawrence says there is "nothing more delightful as a continual walk with God." He writes:

> Please get started now. I don't care how old you are. It is better late than never. I can't imagine how any faithful person can be satisfied without the practice of the presence of God. For my part, I spend as much time as possible alone with him at the very center of my soul. As long as I am with him I am afraid of nothing, but the least turning away from him is unbearable.

Brother Lawrence knew how to grope for God. Maybe we can all take a page from his book.

Meditation: Practice of the presence of God will be different for each person, and yet at its core it's the same: it means seeking God right where you are. Today, practice being present with God in the midst of your life. Maybe that will happen as you drive to work or wait for your children to come out of school. Maybe it means you'll spend five minutes of silent prayer at your desk at lunch, or at a Holy Hour at your parish church, or over a bubbling pot of soup in your kitchen. Whatever it is, make the space and time to seek out God, who is nearer than you think.

Prayer: Ever-present God, help us to keep our eyes always on you and to never doubt that you are near.

Beyond Belief

Readings: Acts 1:1-11; Eph 1:17-23; Matt 28:16-20

Scripture:
The eleven disciples went to Galilee, to the mountain to which Jesus had ordered them. When they saw him, they worshiped, but they doubted. (Matt 28:16)

Reflection: I was listening to an audio book on my drive home from work recently, and a segment caught my attention. Reading from his work, actor and author Alan Arkin related an experience in which a woman who had just witnessed something spectacular alongside him said, "I refuse to believe it."

> "How can you refuse," I asked. "I don't understand. Either what you saw seemed real or it didn't. "No, I refuse to believe it," she repeated again, but she went on. "Because if I believe this, I'm going to have to believe a lot of other things and I refuse to do that."

As soon as I read today's Gospel, I thought of Alan Arkin. I know. It's quite a juxtaposition, but I think there's a kernel of truth in the way my brain made what felt like a logical leap to me. The disciples probably knew somewhere deep down that if what they were seeing was really true and not just a figment of their imagination, it would mean they would have to give up every preconceived notion and belief they may have held and build their life on something else entirely. What a scary prospect!

It's probably the same for us today, isn't it? We're not un-like those doubtful disciples—or the woman in Arkin's book. Doubt protects us in a way. It allows us to hedge our bets a bit, even if unconsciously.

Meditation: I've always posited that if I truly and completely without any shred of human doubt believed in Jesus the way I am called to believe, I could not help but completely trans-form my life. It might mean giving up things I love. It might mean really difficult choices. It would definitely mean aban-doning safety nets and security blankets. And so, I profess and in my heart I want to believe the way I should, but fear holds back a little piece of me. When will we be ready to give it all to Jesus? Can you shed a small layer of doubt today? Can you let go a little more and stand on the mountain Jesus calls you to without fear and with full commitment?

Prayer: Your words give us comfort, Jesus. You are with us always, and yet we are still fearful. Fill us with faith as you did your first disciples so that we, too, may go out and bring others to you.

Heaven on Earth

Readings: Acts 18:9-18; John 16:20-23

Scripture:
"So you also are now in anguish. But I will see you again, and your hearts will rejoice, and no one will take your joy away from you." (John 16:22)

Reflection: I'm a great one for letting other people dampen my joyful spirit. In fact, one of my favorite songs—one I pull out pretty regularly and play at full blast—is a song called "Joy" by alternative-folk singer-songwriter Lucinda Williams. "You took my joy. I want it back," she wails with her southern twang, and I own it as if it is my personal anthem. And then, usually shortly afterward, I remember that if someone can take my joy with such ease, maybe it wasn't the kind of joy that matters, or maybe it wasn't really joy at all, but rather fleeting self-satisfaction or pride or just a happy event that sparked a momentary flare up of positive feelings.

When we read Jesus' words today, we understand that he's talking about the kind of joy that lasts, the kind that lives so deep within us no one else can find it, no less take it. I want that joy so much it hurts sometimes, but it's not something we can get by working harder or exercising more or eating healthier. That kind of joy comes only through a deep connection with our God, one built on and sustained by a deep reservoir of prayer. If we don't remember who we are and who we belong to, we can be pulled off course by any flash in the pan, but that's not what brings true joy; only true faith can provide that.

Meditation: When was the last time you remember being joyful? Where were you? What was happening around you? How long did it last? Now, when was the last time you met someone who was joyful in the midst of challenge or even sorrow? What do you remember most about that? When we meet someone with the kind of faith that feeds the joy Jesus promises, we know we are in the presence of someone and something special. It just feels different. We sense peace and acceptance, and usually we want it for ourselves because we know that to live in that kind of joy is to live in heaven on earth.

Prayer: God of eternal joy, we hunger for a faith so deep it cannot be shaken, a joy so strong it can never be depleted. Teach us to seek the joy that comes through you, not the momentary happiness the world offers now and then.

Only One Way

Readings: Acts 18:23-28; John 16:23b-28

Scripture:
He began to speak boldly in the synagogue; but when Priscilla and Aquila heard him, they took him aside and explained to him the Way of God more accurately. (Acts 18:26)

Reflection: I don't know about you, but the scene in the first reading today is one that sparks my curiosity. We hear about Apollo, an early evangelist who "taught accurately" about Jesus and had been instructed in "the Way," and yet soon after we are told that he needs further clarity in order to be more accurate in his preaching. I can't help but wonder what Priscilla and Aquila said to him about the Way. I wish I could drop into this story if only for a moment in order to gain some clarity for myself. We could all use a Priscilla and Aquila to pop in on us now and then and reset our course so we don't stray too far from the Way, but few of us are so lucky to receive—or open to receiving—that kind of thought-ful personal correction. And you can imagine how easy it would have been for Apollo to rebuff this married mission-ary couple and send them on their way. So much that could have gone wrong did not. Spirit at work yet again.

The richness of everyday detail in this season's readings from the Acts of the Apostles are just the kind of food for thought we need as we come down from our Easter Alleluia high and edge back toward Ordinary Time, which can never be ordinary in light of all we now know. The Acts of the Apostles remind us of that. In the stories of these first disciples, we find our road map, the Way forward.

Meditation: Early Christians, before they were called Christians, were known as followers of the Way, as we see in today's reading. There's something intriguing and mysterious about that label. When we think of ourselves as Christians, it's easy to shrug it off. We know we're Christians. No explanation necessary. But the Way—what would it mean to describe ourselves as followers of the Way? How would it change the way you define yourself or describe your beliefs? How might it change the way you live out those beliefs? Today, look at yourself as an early follower of the Way, and see if that changes how you act and live.

Prayer: Jesus, you said that you are the Way, the Truth, and the Life. Help us to know the way to you and to be the way for others.

Strength in Numbers

Readings: Acts 1:12-14; 1 Pet 4:13-16; John 17:1-11a

Scripture:
All these devoted themselves with one accord to prayer, together with some women, and Mary the mother of Jesus, and his brothers. (Acts 1:14)

Reflection: In the aftermath of the ascension of our Lord, we see the apostles, along with the Blessed Mother and other women followers, gathered in prayer. In community with one another, in conversation with God, they find their strength. I imagine it also helps them push back fear that must be nipping at their ankles. For the second time in recent weeks, the Lord leaves them. First on the cross, when everything seemed lost, and now through his ascension, when everything seems changed. But still, for all their trust and faith and hope, they are human, and being without Jesus had to be scary. In our own way, we know how that feels. We pray and don't get an answer—or at least not the answer we want. We sit in silence and feel nothing but that annoying itch on our nose, and we feel alone, even though in our heart of hearts we know God is with us. But our human minds, with its cascade of monkeys clamoring for attention and a voice, try to convince us otherwise.

And then we go to Mass, filing into a pew to sit next to a stranger, or perhaps a family member or friend. We pray together, we raise our voices, we shake hands, we receive Jesus in the Eucharist. We do exactly what the apostles and Mary and others did in the upper room. We pray as one, and suddenly we do not feel so alone. We look up and see others filing past us into pews and think, "You too?" We are in this together. We need community, but even more than that, we need communal prayer, where we can feel Jesus in our midst even if we cannot always hear his voice.

Meditation: Notice the difference this week when you pray alone and when you pray in community, whether a rosary or holy hour or Mass. Does it feel different to you? If so, how? Does your parish community inspire you to deeper prayer or more regular spiritual practices? Is there a spiritual program you'd like your parish to begin? Can you help get it started? Maybe it's *lectio divina* or adoration or Liturgy of the Hours. Community is critical.

Prayer: Wherever two or three are gathered in your name, there are you among them. That's what you promised us, Lord. Strengthen our community of faith so that we may lift each other up along the way.

More than a Wish

Readings: Acts 19:1-8; John 16:29-33

Scripture:
"In the world you will have trouble, but take courage, I have conquered the world." (John 16:33)

Reflection: Jesus' words today feel like the understatement of the century: "In the world you will have trouble." Tell us about it. Our world's trouble seems to grow by leaps and bounds with each passing day. We see it on the grand scale of global and national politics and closer to home in our workplaces and communities and families. There is no escaping the trouble this world hands out. It is hard to fathom what some go through or how they go on, when we watch their homes washed away by tsunamis, their families lost through the violence of war, their children dying on the dangerous journey to a safer place. Even for those of us blessed with "first-world problems," the struggle is real. Sure, we joke about how we can't live without our smartphones and our creature comforts, but the reality is that trouble comes to us as well—in the form of illness and job issues, addiction and parenting worries, grief and more. We feel burdened by the trouble this world dishes out and, while we take comfort in Jesus' words of reassurance, we also know that this life takes its toll in the here and now. So, what are we to do? How do we maintain our hope?

"This is what Christian hope is: having the certainty that I am walking toward something that is, not something I hope may be," Pope Francis has said. "This is Christian hope. Christian hope is the expectation of something that has already been fulfilled for each one of us."

Meditation: There's a big difference between believing something deep in your heart and simply wishing something were true. Is your faith a belief or a wish? Do you, in the deepest recesses of your heart, know God without question? Do you hope to get to heaven one day, or, as Pope Francis suggests, is your hope firmly planted in the knowledge that heaven is waiting for you? That's what keeps us from being conquered by this world: We have to live in the hope of what we know awaits us, rather wishing for a dream to come true.

Prayer: Lord of all hopefulness, do not let our hearts become so weighed down by the worries of this world that we lose sight of the very real salvation that awaits us in the next.

Cheerful Surrender

Readings: Acts 20:17-27; John 17:1-11a

Scripture:
"Yet I consider life of no importance to me, if only I may finish my course and the ministry that I received from the Lord Jesus, to bear witness to the Gospel of God's grace." (Acts 20:24)

Reflection: On this memorial of St. Philip Neri, I can't help but think back to my very first visit to Rome. On the last day of my stay, I knew I had time for one more church visit and rushed over to Chiesa Nuova. I made it just in time for Mass and slid into a pew. I had visited so many churches during that solo visit—enough to have many of them blur together or seem non-descript—but this one is seared into my memory for all the right reasons. It wasn't for the sculptures or frescoes, soaring ceilings or flying buttresses. I really couldn't tell you much about the actual physical church where St. Philip Neri spent the last twelve years of his life. I remember the Mass, the feeling of community despite a language and culture barrier, the knowledge that even here, in Rome, I had a home in church.

Philip Neri seems a good fit for today's message from St. Paul about not being too attached to this life but rather to the ministry we are called. Philip lived that daily, bringing together lay people in his Oratory to pray and sing. He was known to be cheerful and kind, funny and deeply spiritual, and, like Paul, trusted completely in God's plan. I'll always have a soft spot for St. Philip Neri thanks to his beautiful church down the road from my Roman hotel and the spirituality he left behind there for all who take the time to pause and say a prayer.

Meditation: "There is nothing more dangerous to the spiritual life than to wish to rule ourselves after our own way of thinking," St. Philip Neri once said. We cannot cling to our own ideas, our own plans, our own goals. We have to let go and, like Paul in today's first reading, not worry so much about this life. That's no small challenge. It takes more than determination and commitment; it takes prayer and a willingness to surrender. We can look to St. Philip Neri as a model of the humility and faithfulness, cheerfulness and prayer that will sustain us in our efforts. Make a note to look up St. Philip Neri's life story; reflect on some of his most famous quotes.

Prayer: We surrender our hearts to you, Lord. Help us to do so with courage, with cheer, with patience, and with faithfulness. Jesus, we trust in you.

Truth or Consequences

Readings: Acts 20:28-38; John 17:11b-19

Scripture:
"Consecrate them in the truth. Your word is truth." John 17:17

Reflection: Truth has never been a relative thing. It is what it is. In a world where relativism is rampant—from the political arena to personal life—truth is one thing not up for debate, although you'd never know it these days. People in the public eye put "spin" on just about everything that hits the news media. Ordinary people, myself included, talking about living "my truth." When the truth becomes something we mold to our own wants and desires, we start heading toward trouble. In both the first reading and the Gospel today, truth is the focal point—not truth as we would have it, but the Truth as incarnated in Jesus, the Truth that God has revealed to us.

Even to St. Paul, it was evident that truth could become a tricky matter. In the first reading, he warns that people from within their newly formed Christian community would come forward "perverting the truth" to try to lead people away from those who followed Jesus. Why should our world be any different? Truth often must exist in tension with the human need for power, control, and material riches. The only way to be sure we are not creating a truth in our own image is to cling to the Truth of the Gospel, to keep our eyes focused on Jesus, who reminds us that he is "the way, the truth, and the life."

Meditation: St. Teresa of Avila, Doctor of the Church, wrote, "Truth suffers, but never dies." Reflect on that statement today. As you go through your day, notice where truth may be suffering. Do you have a part in it? What can you do to end the twisting of truth in your own world and in the larger world? While we may not have the power to right the mis-truths at the highest levels, we can begin where we are and effect powerful change—even if it's just on social media or in the office or around our kitchen table. If each one of us protects and promotes the truth, we will soon find that our truth and the Truth become aligned and inseparable, and then all will be right with our world.

Prayer: Jesus, your Truth is not always easy to live, but we know it is the only way to live. Show us the Way to the Truth that sets us free.

Devil's Playground

Readings: Acts 22:30; 23:6-11; John 17:20-26

Scripture:
. . . and the group became divided. For the Sadducees say that there is no resurrection or angels or spirits, while the Pharisees acknowledge all three. (Acts 23:7b-8)

Reflection: Satan is the great divider. Have you ever noticed that when people start getting closer to the truth, maybe when you yourself have edged precariously close to some breakthrough in your own life, out of the blue comes a road-block or figurative explosion that threatens to derail every-thing? The devil loves to sow doubt and division, especially among those striving daily to do God's work. So often people of great faith—deeply committed to their beliefs and their efforts to make the world a better place—end up at each other's throats over differences in opinion. That is not God's work, you can be sure.

I've seen it unfold right before my eyes working in the Church. Everyone is united behind a cause, the fight for the dignity of life, for example. Suddenly, infighting begins over how best to move the cause forward or what to do with Catholics who support moral evil, and now the focus is turned away from the most vulnerable, the ones who need our attention most, and onto our new "enemy," the ones who won't do as we say as soon as we say in the way that we say within our own Church. When you see that happening, take a step back and know that, like Paul, you are watching the devil desperately trying to undo the Lord's work. The devil won't win in the end, but many of us may get caught in the spiritual crossfire. Be on watch.

Meditation: People often joke about the two things you should never discuss in polite company: religion and politics. How sad that talking about God can cause such strong negative reactions on all sides of a conversation. Have you found yourself in such a discussion any time recently? Did anything good come of it? Were any minds changed or did even great division and resentment result? The next time you see division rising up among believers, take a step back and notice if the division is a distraction or a dire need. If it's the former, make a decision not to participate in the mudslinging and instead do something positive—pray, write a letter, call a friend, turn off your phone and silently talk to God.

Prayer: Today we pray for patience and an open mind. May we be forces for unity and work to heal the divisions that tear families, communities, churches apart.

Worth Repeating

Readings: Acts 25:13b-21; John 21:15-19

Scripture:
He said to him the third time, "Simon, son of John, do you love me?" Peter was distressed that he had said to him a third time, "Do you love me?" and he said to him, "Lord, you know everything; you know that I love you." (John 21:17)

Reflection: Poor Peter. He so often seems to be at the wrong end of the questions and answers with Jesus. And although on the surface today's Gospel exchange could seem a little cruel and unusual on Jesus' part, what with the repeated asking of the same question, with 20/20 hindsight we know that Peter needed this opportunity to unravel what he had done on Good Friday. Then three denials; today three affirmations. It's almost like Jesus is giving him the chance to roll back the clock for a do-over. For every time Peter said a variation of, "I tell you, I do not know the man," today he says, "You know that I love you," even as Jesus alludes to the martyr's death he will die in Jesus' name.

Wouldn't we all like an opportunity to unravel or rewind our past mistakes—words said in haste, actions done without thinking of others' feelings, silence when we should have spoken up? Or maybe there have been times when we were in the other position, the one who could offer someone the chance to change a trajectory, offer an apology, or recast a statement gone wrong. Jesus chose Peter, knew he would deny him, even referred to him as Satan at one point, and still Jesus trusted that Peter would do what needed to be done, and Peter trusted that Jesus was who he said he was.

Meditation: What does today's Gospel bring up for you? Do you feel yourself tensing up as Jesus asks Peter over and over to affirm his love, or does this interplay between Master and follower comfort you and remind you that you, too, will be given the same opportunity to make up for past faults, to reclaim your place in the kingdom? Like Peter, we may feel distressed and confused in the face of what we thought were easy answers, but God reassures us that no matter what we do, he remains at our side. And always God gives us another chance, allowing us to repent and reaffirm our love.

Prayer: God of mercy, we come to you with heads bowed, hearts heavy, asking forgiveness for those times we denied you through words or actions or inaction. Hear us as we answer as Peter did. You know that we love you.

Racing toward Heaven

Readings: Acts 28:16-20, 30-31; John 21:20-25

Scripture:
When Peter saw him, he said to Jesus, "Lord, what about him?" Jesus said to him, ". . . What concern is it of yours?" (John 21:21-22)

Reflection: Jealousy and rivalry, topped off with insecurity and fear—so much pours out in Peter's brief exchange with Jesus today. It all sounds so familiar though, doesn't it? We've been there ourselves, in the workplace, in our families, among friends. We don't just worry about how we're doing; we worry about how everyone else is doing. We have a hard time measuring our own progress without making comparisons, without—like Peter in the Gospel—turning around to see who or what is gaining on us. "What about him?" we cry, even if only internally, when we're asked to take on more work and the person next to us is not. "What about her?" we whine when a sibling gets out of taking on some responsibility. We keep a laundry list of slights that make us feel we're not being treated fairly. To that Jesus says, "What concern is it of yours?"

If you've ever been in a race, you know the worst thing you can do for your own speed and form is to turn around again and again to watch the progress of those behind you.

Even the quickest glance can break the momentum. We don't need to track how well others are doing on the spiritual journey; we just need to keep our eyes straight ahead and trained on our own goal. We are each on our own path. The only thing that is the same for each of us is the starting point Jesus gives us: "You follow me."

Meditation: When was the last time you experienced that "What about him?" feeling? Once you got past the initial complaint, did it make you feel any better about your own situation? Did questioning someone else's situation help you get where you needed to go faster or more successfully? Probably not. We tend to be at our best when we stay in our own lane and focus on our own work—spiritual and otherwise. When we do that, with our eyes always on Jesus, all the other pieces fall into place and suddenly we don't see others as competition but as brothers and sisters.

Prayer: Teach us mercy and patience, Lord, as we continue on this journey. Let us not get caught up in the worldly race to win earthly prizes but on the good race that leads to heaven.

Signs of the Spirit

Readings: Vigil: Gen 11:1-9 or Exod 19:3-8a, 16-20b or Ezek 37:1-4 or Joel 3:1-5; Rom 8:22-27; John 7:37-39. Mass during the day: Acts 2:1-11; 1 Cor 12:3b-7, 12-13; John 20:19-23

Scripture:
And they were all filled with the Holy Spirit and began to speak in different tongues, as the Spirit enabled them to proclaim. (Acts 2:4)

Reflection: The Spirit is everywhere today—in wind and tongues of fire, in breath and spoken words. If we let ourselves sink into the first reading, we can imagine the house shaking from wind, as perhaps we've experienced in an especially violent storm. We can almost hear the cacophony of different languages being spoken all at once, as we might in the midst of a popular tourist site in a foreign country. Our senses are overwhelmed by all that is happening when the Spirit enters the scene today. How interesting, then, that for us to truly know the Spirit we must create just the opposite scenario: a still, quiet place where even the slightest whisper can be heard. We'd probably prefer it if the Spirit came to us in a dramatic light show. It would be easier to recognize, easier to believe.

On this Pentecost, we're likely not going to find ourselves speaking in tongues or caught in a windstorm of spiritually epic proportions. More likely, we will have to look for the Spirit amid the ordinariness of our daily lives, but, to be sure, the Spirit is there, waiting for an entry point, hoping we will slow down long enough for the movement to catch us up and propel us forward. Sometimes that might happen in prayer, but, often, it will happen when we are going about our chores and responsibilities. A friend of mine calls those moments God-incidences, and they're all around us, all the time.

Meditation: Sit in silent prayer today for at least five minutes. Turn off all electronics. Sit in a chair or on a cushion, kneel in a pew in a church, or walk down a path through the woods, whatever suits you. Breathe deeply and put yourself in the presence of God. Whenever your mind begins to drift, gently bring it back. Invite the Spirit into your heart. Don't speak any words; just silently listen for what Spirit is asking. Can you do this once a day, or at least once a week? As we end this journey through the Easter season, make a commitment to keep this prayer practice going in the weeks and months ahead.

Prayer: Come, Holy Spirit, fill the hearts of your faithful and kindle in them the fire of your love. Send forth your Spirit and they shall be created. And you shall renew the face of the earth.

References

Introduction
Macrina Wiederkehr, *The Flowing Grace of Now: Encountering Wisdom through the Weeks of the Year* (Notre Dame, IN: Sorin Books, 2019), week one.

April 21: Tuesday of the Second Week of Easter
Henri J.M. Nouwen, *The Only Necessary Thing: Living a Prayerful Life* (New York: Crossroad, 2007), 128.

April 23: Thursday of the Second Week of Easter
Flannery O'Connor, "A Temple of the Holy Ghost," in *A Good Man Is Hard to Find and Other Stories* (Orlando: Harcourt, 1955), 95. Available at https://biblio.csusm.edu/sites/default/files/reserves/a_temple_of_the_holy_ghost_pgs._461-471.pdf.

April 24: Friday of the Second Week of Easter
Pope Francis, General Audience, June 28, 2017, https://w2.vatican.va/content/francesco/en/audiences/2017/documents/papa-francesco_20170628_udienza-generale.html.

April 28: Tuesday of the Third Week of Easter
St. Hildegard of Bingen, *A Feather on the Breath of God* (Hyperion Records, April 1985), CD booklet, page 2.

April 30: Thursday of the Third Week of Easter
Thomas Keating, Theophane Boyd, William Meninger, and Joseph Boyle, *Sundays at the Magic Monastery: Homilies from the Trappists of St. Benedict's Monastery* (New York: Lantern Books, 2002), 72.

May 2: Saint Athanasius, Bishop and Doctor of the Church
Dorothy Day, "Notes by the Way," *The Catholic Worker*, January 1944.

May 4: Monday of the Fourth Week of Easter
Anne Lamott, *Bird by Bird: Some Instructions on Writing and Life* (New York: Anchor Books, 1994), 22.

The Cloud of Unknowing (Brewster, MA: Paraclete Press, 2006), chapter 32.

May 6: Wednesday of the Fourth Week of Easter
Leonard Cohen, "Anthem," *The Future* (Columbia Records, 1992).

May 8: Friday of the Fourth Week of Easter
Thomas Merton, *New Seeds of Contemplation* (New York: New Directions Publishing, 1961), 297.

May 11: Monday of the Fifth Week of Easter
Teresa of Avila, *The Interior Castle*, tr. E. Allison Peers (New York: Doubleday, Image Books edition, 1961), 18.

May 15: Friday of the Fifth Week of Easter
C.S. Lewis, *How to Be a Christian: Reflections and Essays* (New York: Harper One, 2018), 127–28.

May 20: Wednesday of the Sixth Week of Easter
Bernard Bangley, ed., *Nearer to the Heart of God: Daily Readings with the Christian Mystics* (Brewster, MA: Paraclete Press, 2005), 4.

May 21 (Thursday) or May 24: The Ascension of the Lord
Alan Arkin, *Out of My Mind* (Audible Audiobook, 2018), Chapter 3, 5:20 minutes.

May 22: Friday of the Sixth Week of Easter
Lucinda Williams, "Joy," *Car Wheels on a Gravel Road* (Mercury Records, 1998).

May 25: Monday of the Seventh Week of Easter
Pope Francis, *On Hope* (Chicago: Loyola Press, 2017), 64.

May 26: Saint Philip Neri, Priest
Elizabeth Scalia, "St. Philip Neri: How to Pursue Sainthood in 25 Pithy Lines," Aleteia, Dec. 29, 2015: https://aleteia.org /2015/12/29/st-philip-neris-advice-for-a-spiritually -profitable-2016/.

May 27: Wednesday of the Seventh Week of Easter
The Order of Carmelites, "Teresa Avila Quotes," https://ocarm .org/en/content/ocarm/teresa-avila-quotes.